Be The Sky's the Limit

by Barbara A. Donovan

Harcourt
SCHOOL PUBLISHERS

COVER Underwood & Underwood/Corbis; 3 Bob Burch/Jupiterimages; 4 Getty Images; 5 Bettmann/Corbis; 6 Corbis; 7 Getty images; 8 Chuck Eckert/Alamy; 9 Image by Underwood & Underwood/Corbis; 10 Getty images; 11 SHOMBURG CENTER/Art Resource; 12 James Cheadle/Alamy; 13 The Granger Collection, New York.

Copyright © by Harcourt, Inc.

All rights reserved. No part of this publication may be reproduced or transmitted in any form or by any means, electronic or mechanical, including photocopy, recording, or any information storage and retrieval system, without permission in writing from the publisher.

Requests for permission to make copies of any part of the work should be addressed to School Permissions and Copyrights, Harcourt, Inc., 6277 Sea Harbor Drive, Orlando, Florida 32887-6777. Fax: 407-345-2418.

HARCOURT and the Harcourt Logo are trademarks of Harcourt, Inc., registered in the United States of America and/or other jurisdictions.

Printed in the United States of America

ISBN 10: 0-15-351081-1
ISBN 13: 978-0-15-351081-6

Ordering Options
ISBN 10: 0-15-350603-2 (Grade 6 On-Level Collection)
ISBN 13: 978-0-15-350603-1 (Grade 6 On-Level Collection)
ISBN 10: 0-15-357977-3 (package of 5)
ISBN 13: 978-0-15-357977-6 (package of 5)

If you have received these materials as examination copies free of charge, Harcourt School Publishers retains title to the materials and they may not be resold. Resale of examination copies is strictly prohibited and is illegal.

Possession of this publication in print format does not entitle users to convert this publication, or any portion of it, into electronic format.

1 2 3 4 5 6 7 8 9 10   179   12 11 10 09 08 07 06

Ambitious Bessie

Airplanes got better in the years after the Wright brothers' famous 1903 flight. As they improved, interest in airplanes grew. At first, only men flew planes. Then, slowly, women began to fly, too.

There was one group of people who were shut out of flying. They were African Americans. No person of color anywhere in the world—male or female—was a licensed pilot until 1921. That's when a talented, determined, and proud Bessie Coleman earned her wings.

3

Bessie Coleman made the most of every chance that life handed to her. She was born in 1892, in Texas. Bessie was the tenth of thirteen children. Her family was poor, but her early life was happy. Her mother, Susan, wanted all of her children to make something of themselves, so she encouraged Bessie and the others to go to school.

When Bessie graduated from her local school, she wanted to continue her schooling. To do this, she got a job and saved her money. By 1910, she had saved enough money to go to a school in Oklahoma where she could learn a trade. Unfortunately, Bessie only had enough money to stay for one semester. Then she packed her bags and returned home.

Because she was a woman and an African American, few jobs were open to Bessie at the time. She could work as a teacher. Her other choice was to take a job as a domestic. She could clean, cook, or do laundry for others. For the time being, Bessie decided she would take in laundry. She scrubbed sheets, towels, clothes, and other things in large steaming tubs in her backyard. Then she hung the heavy wet laundry on lines to dry. Later she ironed it with a heavy flat iron that she heated on a stove. The work was backbreaking, but Bessie was not afraid of hard work.

By 1915, Bessie was ready to make a move. Her older brother Walter had a well-respected job working on trains that traveled out of Chicago. Walter invited Bessie to join him in the North. Their brother John lived there, too. Bessie decided to take a chance. She packed her bags once again and headed for Chicago.

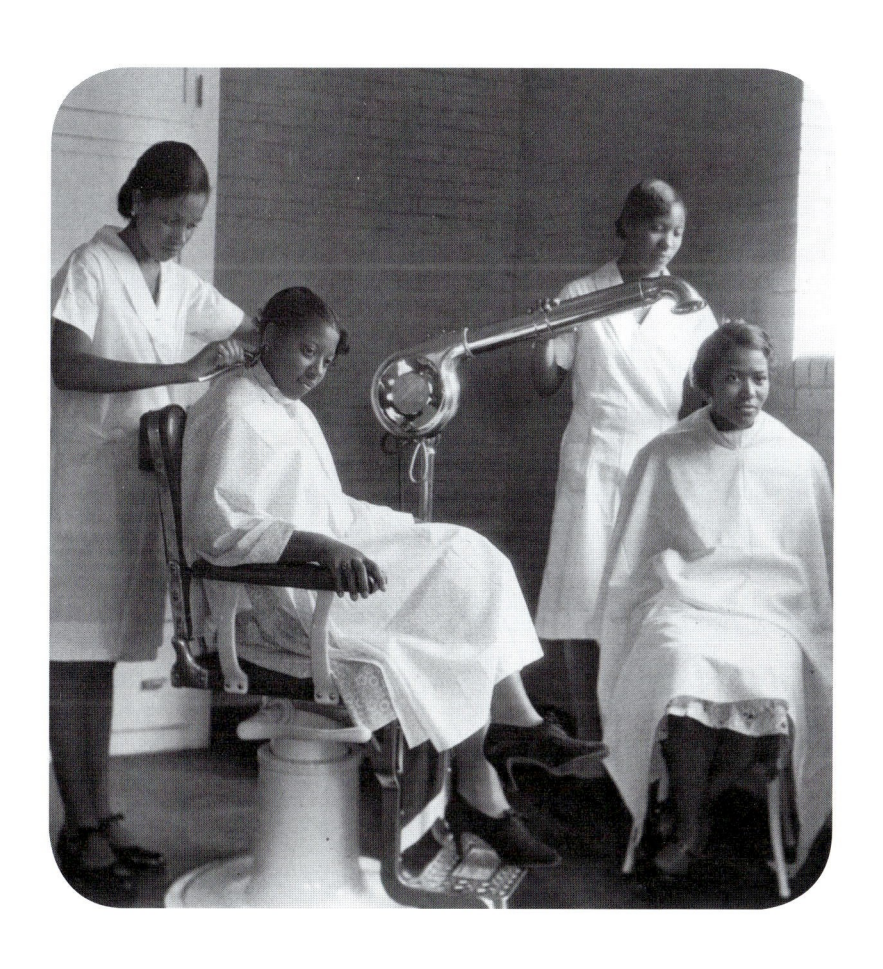

Determined Bessie

Bessie saw her move as a chance to fulfill her mother's dream that she amount to something. As a result, Bessie refused to continue doing other people's laundry. She didn't want to clean their homes or cook for them either. Instead, she worked in a hair salon.

Two years after Bessie moved to Chicago, the United States went to war. Both Walter and John sailed to France to fight in World War I. Luckily, both returned home safely.

    World War I was the first war in which fighting occurred not only on land and sea, but in the sky. The airplanes that military pilots flew were not replicas of the Wright brothers' 1903 plane. Years of work since then had improved aircraft. Still, pilots steered their planes with a stick like a thick baseball bat and a rudder board under their feet. It took skill and courage to fly this kind of plane made of cloth, sticks, and sometimes even cardboard.

When John returned to Chicago after the war, he often told Bessie about the women in France. French women had careers. Some were even pilots. John's stories exerted pressure on Bessie to do something with her life. She was now twenty-seven years old. At last, she knew what she would do. She would learn how to fly. At first, she looked for an African American flight instructor. There were none. As a result, Bessie applied to flight schools run by white pilots. Few of those schools accepted women students. None of them would teach an African American.

Bessie refused to take *no* for an answer. A friend of hers was a publisher named Robert Abbott. He encouraged her to save her money, take French lessons, and then travel to France to get her pilot's license. He believed that in France, the color of her skin would not prevent her from reaching her dream. He was right.

Bessie receives a bouquet from Captain Edison C. McVey.

In November of 1920, Bessie sailed across the ocean to reach for the skies. At her flight school, she learned basics such as taking off and landing. She learned how to stabilize her plane in the air. In addition, she learned how to perform tricks in the air. She learned how to manage the plane's energy to do loops and spins.

Daring Bessie

As dangerous as flying was, Bessie loved it. She had found the one thing in life that made her happiest. On June 15, 1921, Bessie Coleman received her pilot's license. She was the first person of color in the world to earn one. After a few more months of training, Bessie finally returned to the United States.

Bessie's return was joyous. Her accomplishment made headlines. Still, she was not able to find a job flying. Finding a job flying passengers was rare in those days. In 1921, the best a pilot could hope for was a job in a flying circus as a *barnstormer*.

Barnstormers would fly over a town looking for a likely place to land their planes. Often they would fly into a farmer's field. Their scheme was to park their delicate planes and sleep in the farmers' barns. Then they would charge people a quarter or half-dollar to watch them do astounding tricks.

   The tricks these pilots did, such as walking on the wings of their flying planes, were beyond what Bessie had learned. As a result, she headed back to Europe. If she wanted to fly, she had to have more training on trick flying. Bessie was keen to make her name as a pilot. She also had another dream. She wanted to open a flight school. She dreamed that her school would open up the skies to African Americans.

One year later, Bessie had completed her training, and she returned to the United States. Reporters interviewed her for their papers upon her arrival. Robert Abbott sponsored an air show in New York. Bessie would make her first public flight in the United States at the air show. On September 3, 1922, Bessie Coleman flew over the crowd at Glenn Curtiss Field in Garden City on Long Island. She became the first African American woman to fly a plane in public.

Afterwards, she went back home to Chicago. As wonderful as it had been to perform for the first time in the United States, Bessie was thrilled to show off to her hometown crowd. She planned different routines for her hometown air show. Bessie thrilled the audience with stunts that included a figure eight. Then she and the other pilots in the show gave rides to passengers. By evening, it was too dark to fly, and the show disbanded.

Bessie continued performing in air shows around the country. She added new tricks to her performances. Bessie even rigged her airplane so that another pilot could fly it while she jumped off the wing. She used a parachute to safely land on the ground.

Bessie worked hard as a pilot. She also gave talks around the country. She wanted to inspire African Americans to take to the air. She especially loved visiting schools and talking to children about flying. Children, she knew, would be the future of flight. If she could get them interested in flying, then they might see a future for themselves of unlimited possibilities.

Bessie had had the courage to leave her home to follow her dream. She refused to take no for an answer when others refused to teach her to fly. Queen Bess, as the newspapers began calling her, had done what she had set out to do. She had amounted to something. That something was more than just becoming a stunt pilot. Bessie Coleman was an inspiration to all—the sky was the limit for her dreams.

Think Critically

1. What were five key events in Bessie Coleman's life? List the events in chronological order and show the dates for each.

2. How do you think Bessie Coleman felt when she had to return to Texas after one semester at school in Oklahoma?

3. Why did Bessie Coleman travel to France to learn how to fly?

4. Why was Bessie Coleman's achievement as the first person of color in the world to earn a pilot's license so important?

5. Did you enjoy this book? Why or why not?

Science

France's Climate Bessie Coleman studied in France. What is the climate like in France? Use the Internet or another library resource to learn about various French climates. List your findings on a chart.

School-Home Connection Tell a family member about Bessie Coleman. Then talk about how people like Bessie help those who follow after them.

Word Count: 1,344